WORKING TOWARDS
EQUALITY

What Is ABLEISM?

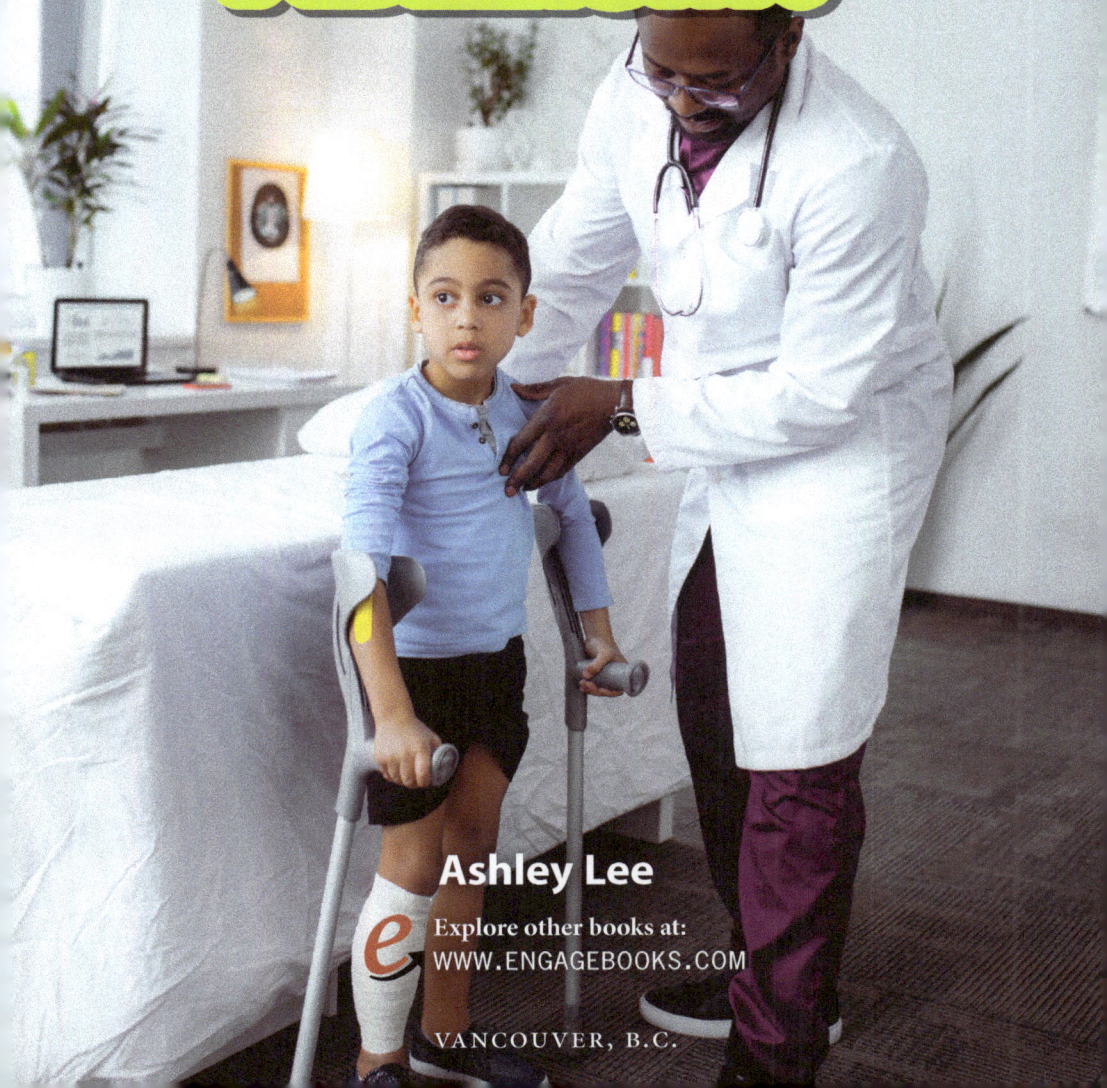

Ashley Lee

Explore other books at:
WWW.ENGAGEBOOKS.COM

VANCOUVER, B.C.

e→ WWW.ENGAGEBOOKS.COM

What Is Ableism? - Working Towards Equality: Level 3
Lee, Ashley 1995 –
Text © 2023 Engage Books
Design © 2023 Engage Books

Edited by: A.R. Roumanis, Ashley Lee, and Melody Sun
Design by: Mandy Christiansen

Text set in Montserrat Regular.
Chapter headings set in Merlo Neue.

FIRST EDITION / FIRST PRINTING

LIBRARY AND ARCHIVES CANADA CATALOGUING IN PUBLICATION

Title: What is ableism? / Ashley Lee.
Names: Lee, Ashley, 1995- author.
Description: Series statement: Working towards equality

Identifiers: Canadiana (print) 20230505538 | Canadiana (ebook) 20230505546
ISBN 978-1-77476-855-6 (hardcover)
ISBN 978-1-77476-856-3 (softcover)
ISBN 978-1-77476-857-0 (epub)
ISBN 978-1-77476-858-7 (pdf)
ISBN 978-1-77878-127-8 (audio)

Subjects:
LCSH: Discrimination against people with disabilities—Juvenile literature.

Classification: LCC HV1568 .L44 2023 | DDC J305.9/08—DC23

This project has been made possible in part by the Government of Canada.

Canada

Contents

4   What Is a Disability?

6   Kinds of Disabilities

8   What Is Ableism?

10 The History of Ableism 1

12 The History of Ableism 2

14 Why Are Some People Ableist?

16 What Does Ableism Look Like?

18 What to Do if You See
    or Experience Ableism 1

20 What to Do if You See
    or Experience Ableism 2

22 Superheroes Against
    Ableism in the Past

24 Superheroes Against
    Ableism Today

26 Ways to Support Change 1

28 Ways to Support Change 2

30 Quiz

What Is a Disability?

A disability is when someone's body or mind works in a different way than most people's. It can make it harder for them to do certain things. Some disabilities can be seen and some cannot.

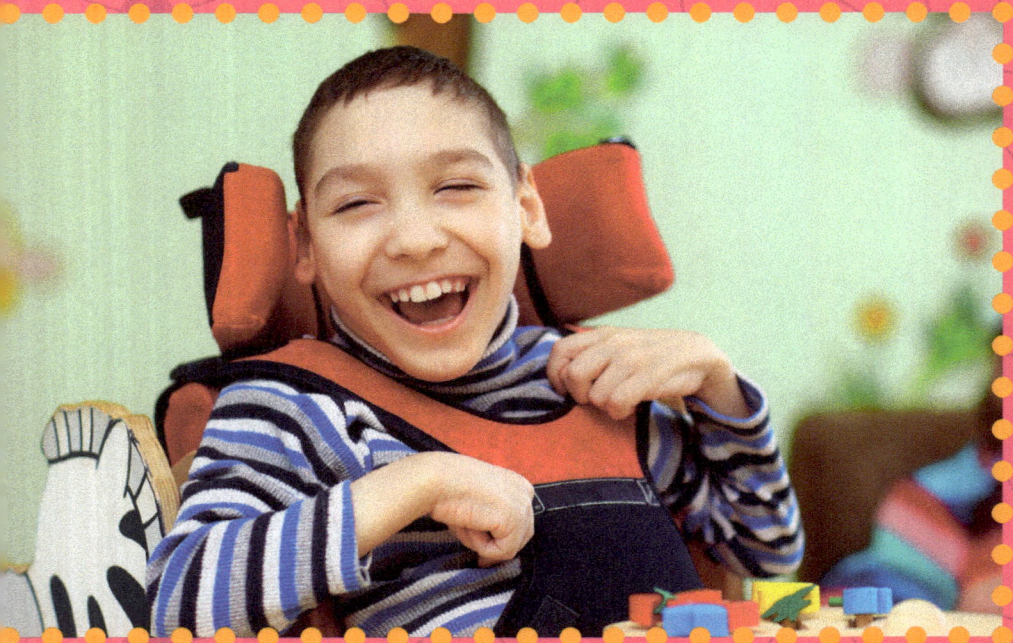

Some disabilities only last a short amount of time. Others last forever. Someone may be born with a disability or they may get a disability later in life.

About 1.3 billion people around the world have a disability.

Kinds of Disabilities

There are many different kinds of disabilities that affect different areas of the body or mind. Some people may have trouble controlling their body. They may not be able to see or hear.

Other people may have trouble learning or communicating with other people. They may have a hard time controlling their emotions. Some disabilities affect a person's memory.

What Is Ableism?

Ableism is when people treat others unfairly because they have a disability. It means not giving everyone the same chances or opportunities. People with disabilities are often **excluded** from places and activities.

KEY WORD

Excluded: to keep someone or something out.

Some people who are ableist think they are better than people with disabilities. They think people who are different are bad. Some people think people with disabilities need to be fixed.

The History of Ableism 1

During the Middle Ages, it was thought that people with disabilities were being punished by God. People with disabilities were often harmed. Sometimes people with disabilities were kept in cages.

In the 1800s and early 1900s, people with disabilities were often sent to special hospitals called asylums. These hospitals were supposed to help them. The hospitals often treated them poorly instead.

11

The History of Ableism 2

In the late 1800s and early 1900s, many people believed that people with disabilities should not have children. They believed disabilities came from bad **genes** and only people with good genes should have children. This belief was called eugenics.

KEYWORD

Genes: traits that are passed down from one family member to another.

The disability rights movement is a group of people fighting for the rights of people with disabilities. It became popular in the 1960s and 1970s. Their hard work led to laws protecting the rights of people with disabilities in several countries.

DISABILITY RIGHTS ARE HUMAN RIGHTS

Today, only about 45 countries have laws that protect people with disabilities.

Why Are Some People Ableist?

Some people are ableist because they see other people being ableist. This makes them think it is okay. Others may believe people with disabilities cannot do the same things non-disabled people can do.

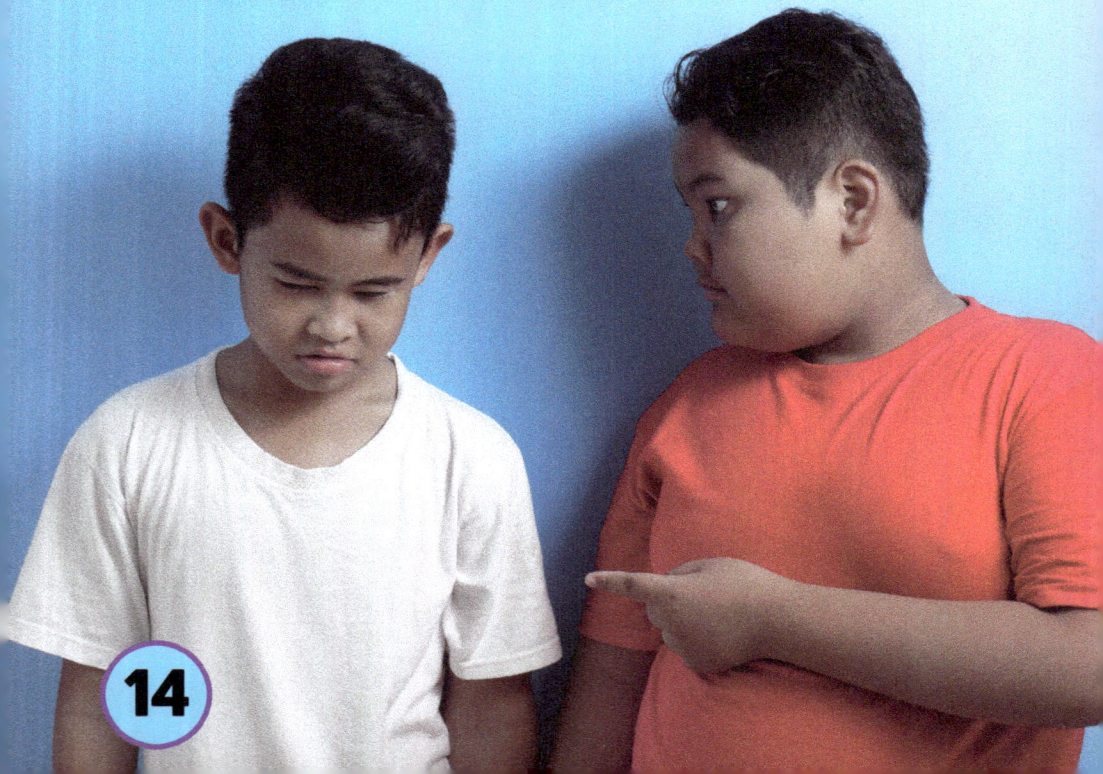

Some people may act ableist because they do not understand what it is like to be different or have a disability. They might not know how to treat others with kindness. Sometimes, people fear things they do not understand and this makes them act out.

What Does Ableism Look Like?

Making fun of a person because of their disability is ableist. It is also ableist to leave someone out of activities because of their disability. Ableism also happens when people think someone with a disability cannot do something without giving them a chance to try.

Many things are created in ways that make it hard for people with disabilities to use them. Some buildings only have stairs and do not have a ramp for people in wheelchairs. Some elevators do not have **braille** on the buttons for people with vision loss.

Braille: a way of writing things using raised dots that people read with their fingertips.

17

What to Do if You See or Experience Ableism 1

Stand up against ableism. Some people may not know that what they are doing or saying is ableist. Explain why it is wrong and unfair to treat someone differently because of their abilities.

If you do not feel safe talking to the person who is being ableist, tell a teacher or parent what you saw. They can talk to the person who is being ableist. They can help stop it from happening again.

What to Do if You See or Experience Ableism 2

If someone is ableist towards you, find support. Talk to your friends and family. Having someone to talk to can make you feel better. Your family can help you talk to a **counselor** if you need one.

KEY WORD

Counselor: a person who gives advice to others.

You can also support others who are experiencing ableism. Listen to their story. Let them know they are not alone.

Superheroes Against Ableism in the Past

Eunice Kennedy Shriver's sister had a disability. They grew up playing sports together. Eunice noticed there were not many sports teams her sister could join. Eunice started the Special Olympics in 1968 for people with **intellectual disabilities**.

KEY WORD

Intellectual disabilities: disabilities that affect people's ability to learn and do certain everyday tasks.

Javed Abidi helped make India more **accessible** for people with disabilities. He helped make public spaces and buses easier for people with disabilities to use. He also fought for the creation of laws that protected people with disabilities in India.

Accessible: able to be used by everyone.

Helen Keller was a writer and a teacher who could not see or hear. She worked with the American Foundation for the Blind to teach people about not being able to see. She fought to have people with disabilities taken out of asylums.

23

Superheroes Against Ableism Today

Liz Carr is an English actress and comedian. She has been fighting for the rights of people with disabilities for more than 25 years. She has talked about disability rights on TV and been part of many disability rights **protests**.

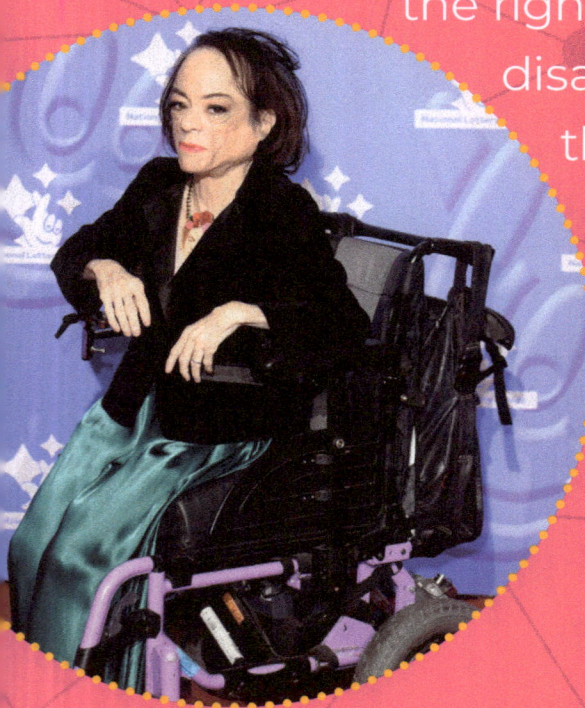

KEY WORD

Protests: when groups of people come together to fight for or against something.

Eddie Ndopu is a disability activist from South Africa. This means he works hard to fight ableism. He works with groups like the United Nations to help create equality for people with disabilities.

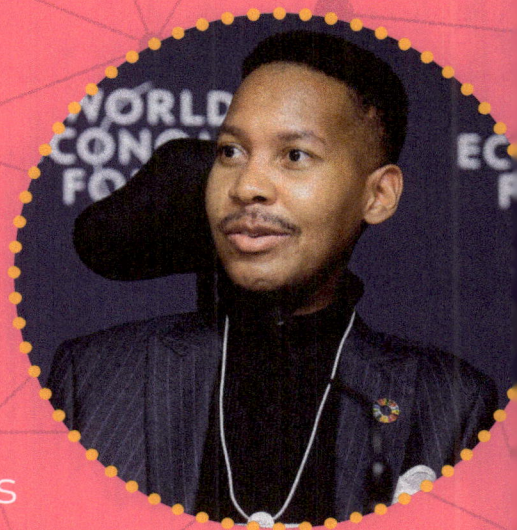

Yetnebersh Nigussie is an Ethiopian lawyer. She started the Ethiopian Centre for Disability and Development (ECDD). The ECDD helps people with disabilities get the services they need. They also fight for the rights of disabled people in Ethiopia.

Ways to Support Change 1 and 2

Learn about different disabilities and how they affect people. This will help you understand what other people are dealing with and how you can best help them if they do need help. Share what you learn with your family and friends.

Treat everyone the same. Do not leave people out just because they have a disability. Include everyone in games and activities.

Ways to Support Change 3 and 4

Talk to teachers or the principal at your school about making things more accessible for people with disabilities. This may mean asking for wheelchair ramps. You could even ask for **audiobooks** in the library for people who have a hard time reading.

KEY WORD

Audiobooks: books that are listened to instead of read.

Do not assume people with disabilities need help. Many people with disabilities learn to do things on their own, even if they have to do them differently than others. It is ableist to think that people need help just because they have a disability.

Quiz

Test your knowledge of ableism by answering the following questions. The questions are based on what you have read in this book. The answers are listed on the bottom of the next page.

1 How many people around the world have a disability?

2 What does the word "excluded" mean?

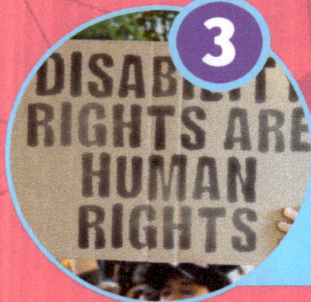

3 How many countries have laws that protect people with disabilities?

4 What is a counselor?

5 Who was Helen Keller?

6 What year did Eunice Kennedy Shriver start the Special Olympics?

Explore Other Level 3 Readers.

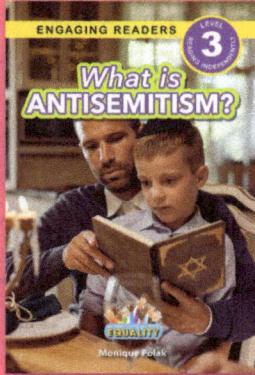

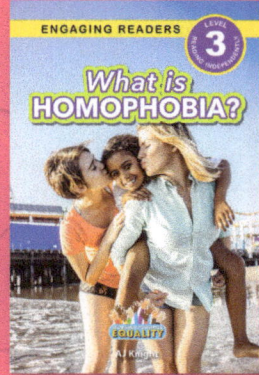

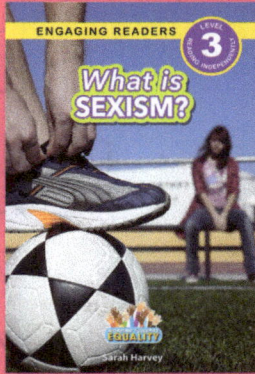

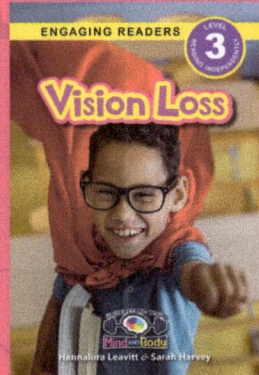

ENGAGING READERS — LEVEL 3
What is AGEISM?
EQUALITY
Sarah Harvey

ENGAGING READERS — LEVEL 3
What is ANTISEMITISM?
EQUALITY
Monique Polak

ENGAGING READERS — LEVEL 3
What is HOMOPHOBIA?
EQUALITY
AJ Knight

ENGAGING READERS — LEVEL 3
What is RACISM?
EQUALITY
Sarah Harvey & Melody Sun

ENGAGING READERS — LEVEL 3
What is SEXISM?
EQUALITY
Sarah Harvey

ENGAGING READERS — LEVEL 3
Diabetes
Mind and Body
Kit Caudron-Robinson

ENGAGING READERS — LEVEL 3
Obesity
Mind and Body
Kit Caudron-Robinson

ENGAGING READERS — LEVEL 3
Autism
Mind and Body
AJ Knight

ENGAGING READERS — LEVEL 3
Vision Loss
Mind and Body
Hannalora Leavitt & Sarah Harvey

Visit www.engagebooks.com/readers

www.ingramcontent.com/pod-product-compliance
Lightning Source LLC
Chambersburg PA
CBHW051241020426

42331CB00016B/3475